MW01715385

One Teaspoon of Home

DESI FOOD POETRY

Noor Ali

MARKINGS
PUBLISHING

One Teaspoon of Home | Desi Food Poetry by Noor Ali
First published in Pakistan in 2023 by Markings Publishing

Written by
Noor Ali

Illustrations by
Umme Aimen Kazmi
@quirky_kahaniyan

©All rights reserved.
No part of this publication may be reproduced or used in any form or by any means graphic, electronic or mechanical including photocopying, recording, taping or information storage and retrieval system - without written permission of Markings

ISBN: 978-969-9748-24-0

MARKINGS
PUBLISHING

info@markings.com.pk
www.markings.com.pk

Dedication

To shared food memories with friends and family.

From the paandaan of Aapa Ji, or 80s birthday parties where fruit chaat was part of the standard menu, or having dahi bhallay in Liberty Market, or going with Mehar and Dolly to Regal for aloo tikkis and chai in the car, or Ammi and Tariq bhai deciding on the excellent idea of falooda or aana (penny) kabab late at night, or drinking tha with bhaiya's kababs in Model Town, or a curvy ice cream cone from Robiya with cousins, or gol guppay at the entrance of Bagh-e-Jinnah, or the karary paapar from the sides of the trails inside the park, or a paper cone filled with warm channay, or a little plastic bag with chikkar cholay, or falsay ka sharbat in Anarkali, or gunnay ka rus from any street corner, or bhuttay or singharay cooked under hot sand, or Mamu Ishaq lovingly calling rusk "papay", or Adnan glorifying a warm kulcha for breakfast, or Abu leaving his chai unfinished always- how can one be of Lahore and not be immersed in memories of food?

Food is introduced to us as characters with personality, their quirks, flaws, punches, temperament(taaseer), attitude- overwhelming and underwhelming. We also know that moderation is not a thing- because there is bizarre pleasure in saying that *kha kha key pagal ho gye hain* (we have gone insane from eating), or in Punjabi *dhap dhap phadal* (exhausted and drained with gluttonous consumption), or *thoos gaye hain* (stuffed beyond capacity).

For those of us who live "elsewhere", memories of food bring home a sense of belonging. Food situates our memories of home just like it dots our street corners, rehris, and sidewalks. When it rains, we crave pakoray and gulgulay, in the summer we want to choomp mangoes, and challenge our teeth with ghandariyan and reweriyan in winter, we think of garam garam aanday at cold train stations and look for a thermos of garam chai on road trips. Being Elsewhere we are always in two places, Here and Not There. Not There is where home is, where memories reside, and the palate is stirred. These poems are an ode to those memories- while not all the foods may be our favorites, the memories associated with them are like a familiar hug. I am hopeful that many of my memories will stir some of yours, and that you will find your Not There in them.

Before the poems evoke nostalgia however, they speak about politics and patriarchy, and they speak about the resistance and resilience performed daily in the face of our lives. Food centers us with an intent particularity as our world crumbles around us. We indulge in textures and flavors, and find a grounding within these known symbols.

My gratitude to Mehar, Shima, Kiran, and Samia for taking this food journey with me, opening pathways, and enjoying the ride. Thank you, Aimen for shape shifting the words into pictures that made me fall in love with the work even deeper. Our squeals of laughter at shared memories in two very different spaces was nothing short of magic.

The overwhelming feeling I am left with is that so much was left to be said- kunna, pakoray, hareesa, sajji, koftay, karahi, trifle- there are so many food memories at every corner of home, that the only way to be done was to leave a whole lot unsaid.

Contents

Contents

بریانی

BIRYANI

Is a cross-border identity crisis
forever jumping multiplicities
forever intersectional
Sindhi, Bombay, Malay.
Who would have thought
that potatoes, lemons, cilantro
would participate in warfare
while unground spices provide
oral obstacles to
quick consumption?

جلیبی

JALEBI

Swirls of sweet seduction-
Its gaudy presence
making promises
that it does not deliver
except leaving one
in
a sticky situation.
Who would think an orange, sugar-dripping,
oil-battered one
would have such an attitude of celebration?

ناشتہ

NAASHTA

Behold the bold
orange, pillowy fluff
of halwa
incompetently held in a breaking, flaking puri
that drifts in protest.
Choreograph a sequential performance
between Aloo Channa and Halwa taking turns.
Wash it down in a river of
sweet heady lassi.
Let the froth rise
above you
as you fall.

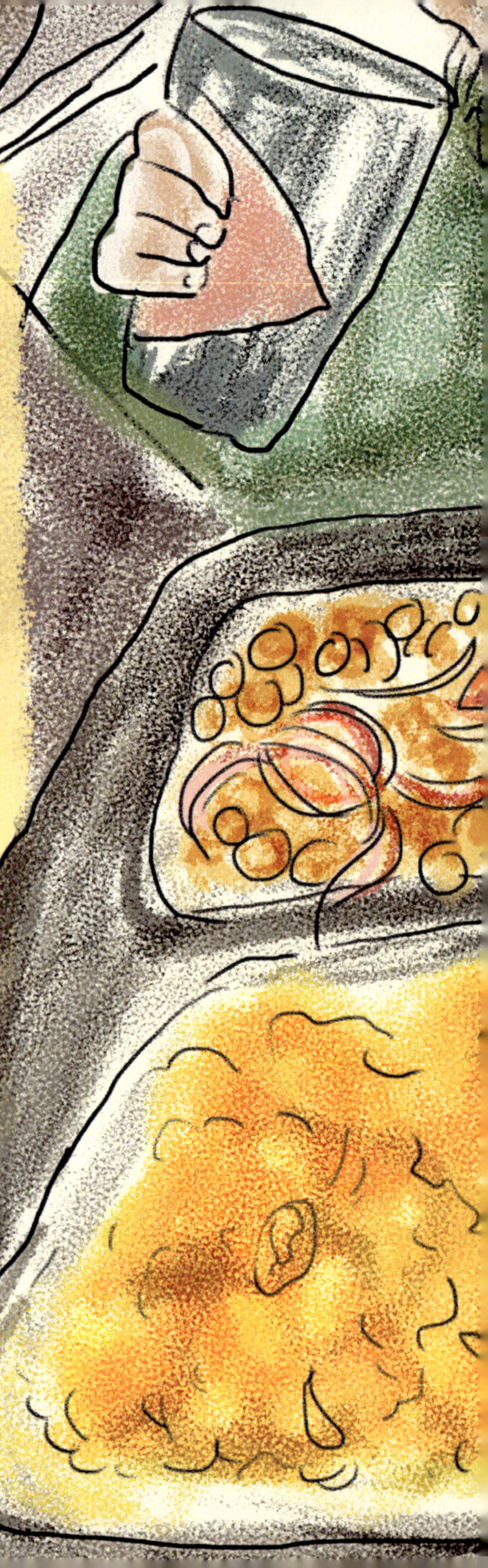

ریگل
نکّڑ کارنر
کوکاکولا

آلو ٹکّی

ALOO TIKKI

You are nothing
if not served on a saucer
(thick, ceramic)
with tea
in a tiny blue teapot
(curvy, metal)
near Regal in Lahore
in a car.
You are nothing
without chutney.
You squished oily potato mush
I love you.

گول گپے

GOLE GUPPAY

What reputation must precede
to have a name
as this?
A celebration of roundness.
A celebration of an airy middle
of profound emptiness
yet a wholeness
fragile, but distinct.
A performative futile drowning in tang and heat
that strains right through
but expects prompt action.

کشمیری چائے

KASHMIRI CHAI

If love was rose-colored-
a warm drink
a play of salt and sugar
a flirtation with pistachio.
It would be you.

CHAI RUSK چائے رسک

If there was a love contest
for natural evening pairings
Chai Rusk would win
the Pakistani heart
over
and over.
Chai Rusk is a national institution
a legacy
passed lovingly down generations.
No one questions chai rusk,
no one casts doubt.
It does not need a welcome.
It is always at home.
It is home.
Shaped like a half planet, or a pack of cards
a mix of smooth
and coarse.
A crunch that is unreluctant, unhesitant, unresistant
in its fateful repeated drowning
unapologetically and quickly soaked,
breaks without disdain,
an edible sponge.
Chai Rusk is an attitude.

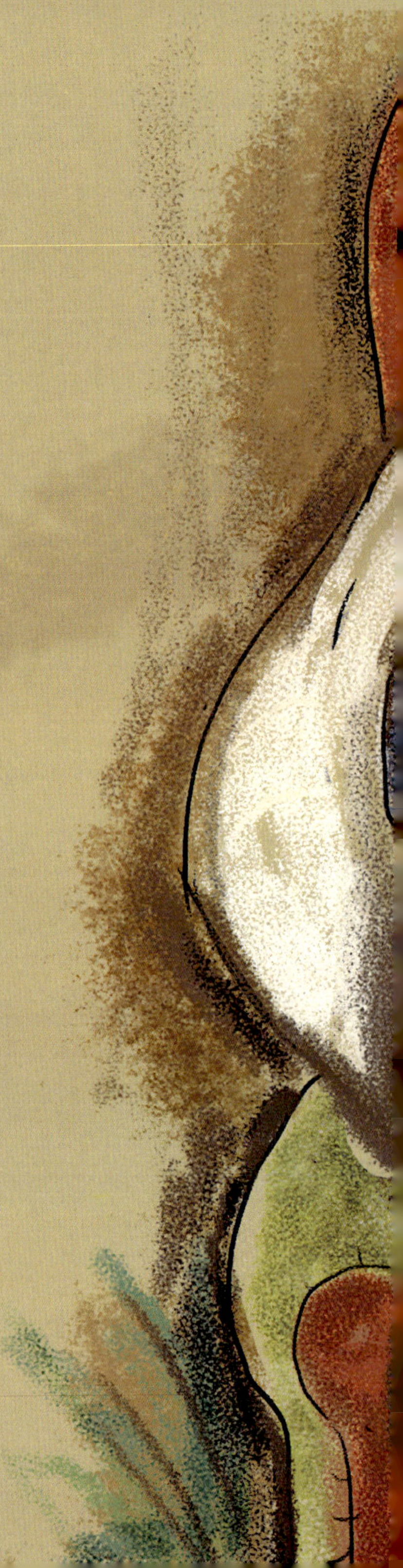

نلی نہاری 650
مغز نہاری 850

نہاری

NIHARI

Is slowness-
A prolonged semi-colon
an elaborated simmer
an intentional exaggeration
to diffuse the edge of flesh
and soften it to a yogic core
except
when you reach the other end
you are ravenous
with the earthly pleasures
of tongue and belly.
A climactic end to failed spirituality.

پان

PAAN

When life wraps itself
in a leaf
with neatly folded, crisp corners
and presents you with options of being
saada, plain
khushbu wala, fragrant
with elements that cause distress
or sweetness
or bitterness.
Choose your elements wisely.

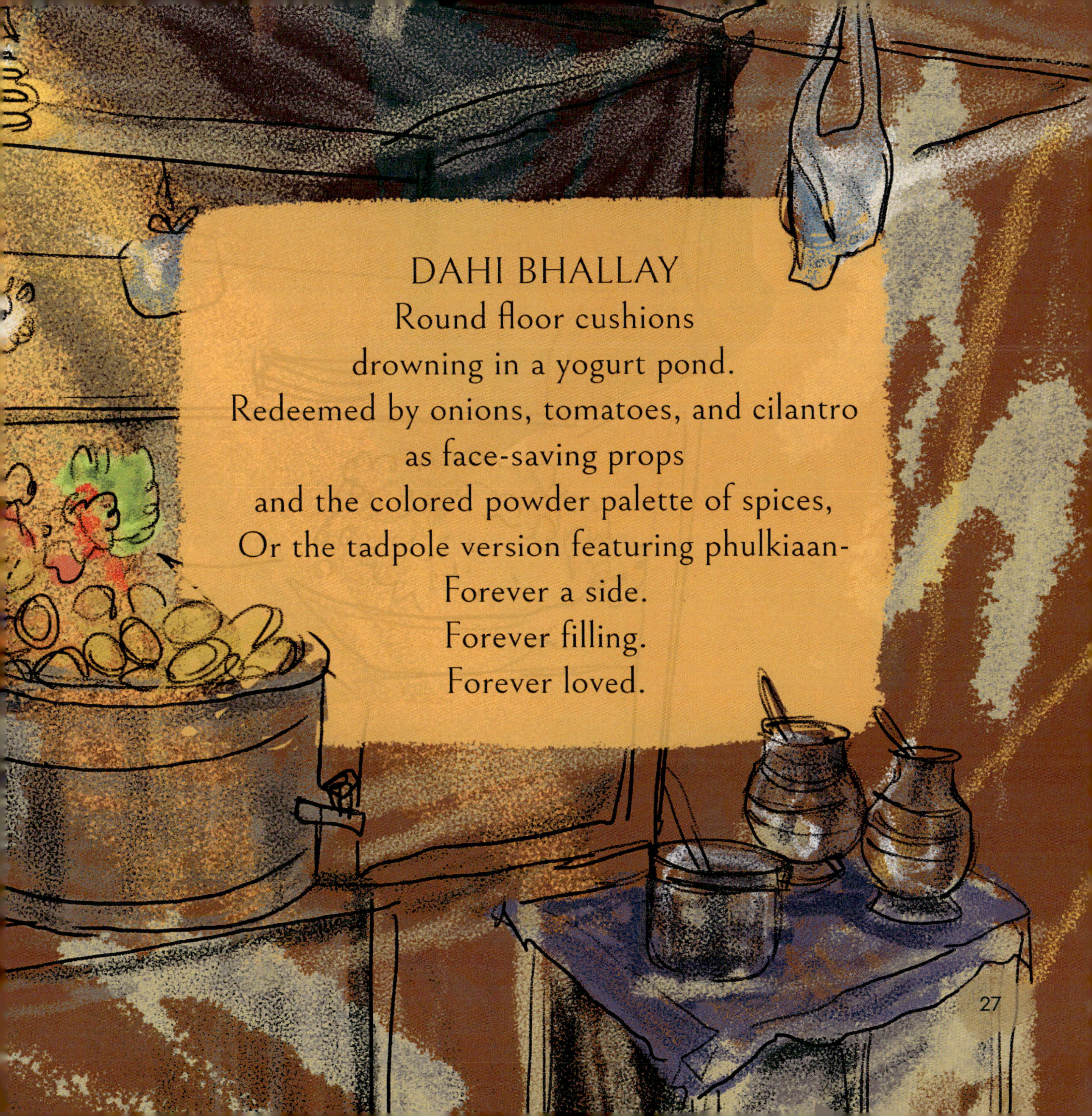

DAHI BHALLAY

Round floor cushions
drowning in a yogurt pond.
Redeemed by onions, tomatoes, and cilantro
as face-saving props
and the colored powder palette of spices,
Or the tadpole version featuring phulkiaan-
Forever a side.
Forever filling.
Forever loved.

ILK
PRODUCT

FALOODA فالودہ

Is an act of sugary politics.
An homage to feminism
and simultaneous shackles of patriarchy.
Like its noodles
that slip and fall
and its frozen heart
that melts without warning.

سیخ کباب

SEEKH KABAB

The epitome of sacrifice.
Oh, to be butchered
and wrapped
around a metal skewer.
Grilled.
Devoured.
A slender ode to gluttony.
A cause for conversion
to carnivorous pleasure.

دال ماش

DAAL MAASH

Like a sunflower
you promise an awakening.
A direction to us wayward souls.
You are lentil
yet, your glories are glorious
and your promise of deliverance
true.

SABIR CHINESS
SOUP & FAST FOOD
SOUPS
Manchu
Sweat and Sour
CHICKEN

چائنیز سوپ

CHINESE SOUP

We are not
Made in China.
we are Made in Pakistan
and kept warm
for cold Lahore days.
Wisps of steam and fog
meeting over sirka and hari mirch, soya sauce,
chicken, corn, and globs of egg.
Transported on a cart with a plexi-glass kitchen.
Pak-cheen taluqaat ka nishaan.

FIRNI فرنی

The only thing sweet about weddings
are the clay–clapped thootis at the end
like the final taalian
at the end of something grandiose
but with earthy elements that seek to humble with simplicity.
Like the thootis are saying "bus ab baith jaaen, khamoshi ke saath",
or
"Apna munh in thoothion ki tarha bund kar lein"
Two full moons
to neatly fit the palms of your hands.
A complete world
held completely
thandi, grainy, earthen to touch
opened to creamy white glossiness
with the simple majesty of crinkled silver
and powdered nutty green.
The best thing about thootis is that there are two.
An indulgent comfort
in the promise of another side.

پائے

PAYE

Why?

An ode to our infatuation with
the body -
siri, kaleji, gurday, paye, maghaz, kapuray.
Head, liver, kidney, hooves, brain, testicles.
Each one an (un)delicate delicacy.
Why?

JOHN PLAYER
GOLD LEAF
تمباکو نوشی کا انجام - گینگرین

چپل کباب

CHAPPAL KABAB

A portal to urban mythology
about men flattening meat patties with their feet
while pancake-sized goodness
oozes with flavor
and stains with oil
the newspaper it was wrapped in
and served on.

فروٹ چاٹ

FRUIT CHAAT

Why do you exist?
Oh, ruiner of love.
Cut fruit is an act
of laborious, intentional love.
But sprinkled with
fart-inducing
chaat masala
is
abuse.

شامی انڈا

SHAAMI ANDA

Everyone knows that an omelet
does not go in a burger
except if it's
from a food cart in Mini Market
smushed to perfection
with the myth of the absent/present shami kabab-
Cooked meat paste with more lentil and potato
than decent folks would acknowledge.
Fried to hide that deception.

انکل گولا
جیلی

GOLA

A glucose rainbow
of crushed ice
swirled to psychedelic
shape shifting
besides Neela Gumbad.
A reminder of temporality
and states of matter
matter of factly.
From solid to liquid
from sweet to bland
from emphatic to dragged and dumped.

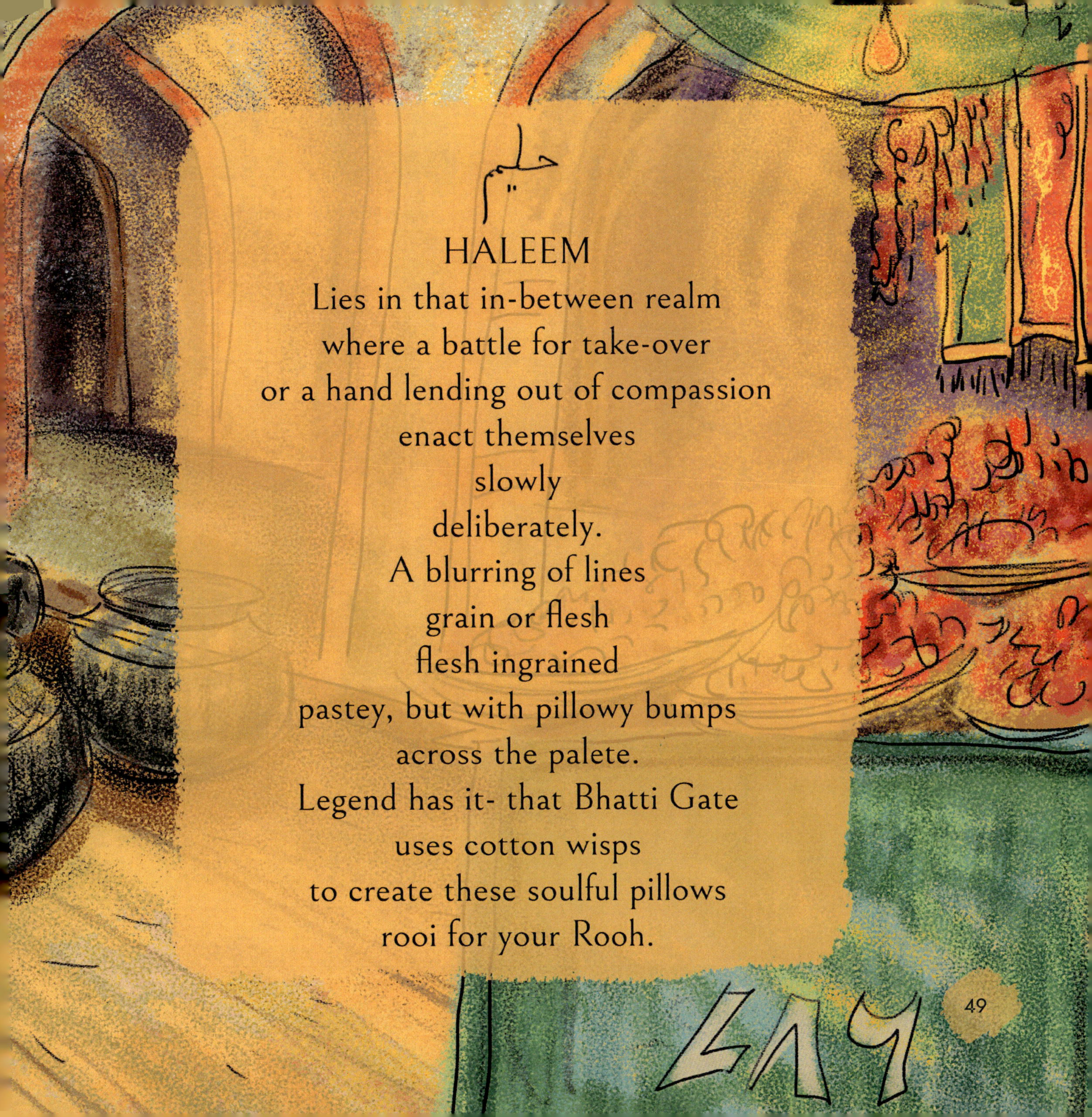

حلیم

HALEEM

Lies in that in-between realm
where a battle for take-over
or a hand lending out of compassion
enact themselves
slowly
deliberately.
A blurring of lines
grain or flesh
flesh ingrained
pastey, but with pillowy bumps
across the palete.
Legend has it- that Bhatti Gate
uses cotton wisps
to create these soulful pillows
rooi for your Rooh.

چانپیں

CHAAMPAEN

There is far too little meat on you
to be taken seriously.
Grossly overrated
like a pakora of the meat industry.
Beckoning to the city of saints
offering a timelessness under a tower of time
delivering little promise
and rubbing it in
with the enormity of what's left behind.

لاھوری کلچہ

بریڈ ہگس

BREAD HUGS

Yaar, I'm avoiding carbs.
Ghar ki garam roti.
Sunrise kulcha with chai to wake up the day.
Buttery garlic roghni naan, sesame settled in knuckle imprinted grooves.
Sweet-heady sheer maal- milk stuff that is royalty personified.
Parathay with swirling spirals pointing to infinite profundities.
Keemay waley naan from Ferozepur Road-
a break apart experience that makes one whole.
Wrap up your light heart in heavy katchori.
Kambakhton, zaalimon- I'm avoiding carbs, na.

شیریں

مٹھائی کی دکان

MITHAI KI DUKAAN

Ascending spiral staircases
of squares and diamonds, rectangles and ovals,
circles rolled and gently patted with that final biometric evidence
that seats an almond.
Behold the burfi- cradle of milk and sugar.
Listen to the loud ladoo- gold speckled celebration of baby boys.
Drown in the brown gulab jamun- squish of syrupy warmth.
Rest on the flaky flat bed of pateesa- an unlayering existential crisis.
Roll on the pillow of fair and lovely ras gullah.
Graze on the glaze of sugary balushahi.
Trip on the tongue festival that only a name like kalakand can give
or build your own almond caliphate with khatai.
Sit in the luxury of sesame-rolled andarasa.
Skip to the beat of tiny chum chum.
Jiggle to the disco rubber of Karachi halwa.
Dream in the cream of ras malai.
Surrender to the massive attitude of petite kaju katli
or place yourself on the rich throne of Sohan halwa.

Made in United States
North Haven, CT
17 September 2023

41662123R00033